True SF Anime

MICHAEL ANDRE-DRIUSSI

ISBN: 1947614088
ISBN-13: 978-1-947614-08-6
****

■■

"'Real SF' Anime for People Who Don't Watch Anime," *New York Review of Science Fiction No. 185*, Jan 2004.

"More 'True SF' Anime for People Who Don't Watch Anime," *New York Review of Science Fiction No. 198*, Feb 2005.

Anime review of feature *The Place Promised in Our Early Days* (dir. Makoto Shinkai), *Internet Review of Science Fiction*, Nov 2005.

"'True SF' Anime — Update 2007," *New York Review of Science Fiction No. 232*, Dec 2007.

Anime review of TV series "The Melancholy of Haruhi Suzumiya," *Internet Review of Science Fiction*, Feb 2008.

Anime review of feature *Paprika* (dir. Satoshi Kon), *Internet Review of Science Fiction*, Aug 2008.

Anime review of TV series *Mushishi* for *New York Review of Science Fiction No. 245*, Jan 2009.

"The Anime Renaissance: 1986 to 2010," *New York Review of Science Fiction No. 278*, Oct 2011.

"My Life with Animation" published here for the first time.

"Apparent Influences in 'Haibane Renmei'" published here for the first time.

"'Planetes': Contrasting the Manga and the Anime" published here for the first time.

CONTENTS

INTRO

First, a few words about my goal for this little book.

I am a life-long reader of science fiction and fantasy. I have also been interested in Japan for a long time: as a teenager I visited Japan, and in my twenties I worked there for two years. I wasn't interested in Japanese animation at that time, but in the 1990s anime went through a high quality upgrade, a renaissance of style and content, and I became hooked. So for ten years now I've been interested in combining these two interests by finding the Japanese animation (or "anime") that best fits with the sense and pleasures of written genre. This is tricky, because anime is a universe all of its own. I seek out stuff that is similar to genre text, which means shouldering aside a lot of anime cliché.

Anime has a large number of genres, including one called "Sci Fi anime." My chief complaint about "Sci Fi anime" is that it is dominated by subgenres involving mecha (powered armor fighting suits), cyberpunk retreads, giant robots, battleships in space, and other tropes for which I have a low tolerance. I'm constantly on the lookout for anime that matches my sense of written SF, and I have to dig through huge piles of stuff to find the occasional pony.

By way of example, so that anime fans can calibrate, allow me to list eight Big Name Sci Fi Anime titles and give notes for why I won't be talking about each:

- *Howl's Moving Castle* (terribly disappointing)
- *Ghost in the Shell* (I don't like it)
- *Akira* (I hate it)
- "Neon Genesis Evangelion" (I can't watch it)
- *Vampire Hunter D* (I can't watch it)
- "Gundam" (I don't like it)
- "Macross" (I can't watch it)
- "Bubblegum Crisis" (I can't watch it)

There is so much Sci Fi Anime that it has many different subgenres: *Ghost in the Shell*, *Akira*, and "Bubblegum Crisis" all fit into Sci Fi Anime's version of cyberpunk; "Evangelion," "Gundam," and "Macross" are part of the "mecha" category (soldiers in mechanical armor). I myself don't like either subgenre. As for my own taste, one anime podcaster has pigeonholed it as "Art House Anime." At times I wish it were true, since then I'd love "Serial Experiment Lain" and "Gankutsuou: The Count of Monte Cristo," but I hate them. (In fact, *Robot Carnival*, something of an Art House Anime standard, turned me off on anime for about ten years.)

I hope this makes plain that I am emphatically not aiming to deliver a "Sci Fi Anime 101." To the contrary, this is a highly idiosyncratic "Anime for SF & F Readers" that strictly applies filters against "Sci Fi Anime" to deliver the good stuff only. How such filtering would interact with American Sci Fi Cinema remains unseen, but I suspect it would fare far worse than anime has.

My Life with Animation

I was waiting in line to see *Star Wars* for the first time in its first run. Despite the seeming paradox, I had already read the book, and I wasn't much impressed by it.

I was with my mother, and we were in Los Angeles. There was a Japanese guy in line behind us, and as we waited in that big line, which was said to be "even bigger than the line for *The Exorcist*," he spoke with us, me in particular. We talked about SF — probably "Star Trek." He asked if I knew mythology. I said I did. He mentioned Perseus, and I rattled off the main points. We had a good time talking, and then he asked my mother if he could give us some free tickets to a Japanese animated movie.

Star Wars turned out to be better than the book, and about a year later I saw the semi-legendary Sanrio movie, *Metamorphoses* (1978), which was somewhat like Disney's *Fantasia* (1940) with original music by the Rolling Stones and the Pointer Sisters. The animation was good but I felt the story, or "stories," were lacking, being more "mood pieces."

I had watched Japanese cartoons as a child. I saw "Kimba the White Lion" and "Marine Boy." By the 1970s I was watching international animation collections on TV, including Will Vinton's claymation work, in addition to unsubbed Japanese shows like "Raideen" broadcast for the Japanese expat community. In the 1980s I was able to drive to art house cinemas like the Nuart in West LA and the Fox in Venice to see animation festivals. I enjoyed features like the Italian *Allegro non Tropo* (1976) and the French *Fantastic Planet* (1973). But from my perspective, there was an increasing gap between art and story, such that one had either weak art for a strong story, like Bakshi's *The Lord of the Rings* (1978), or strong art for a weak story, as in *Heavy Metal* (1981).

The anime anthology feature *Robot Carnival* (1987) was the nadir for me, with strong art supporting poisonous stories. After that I quit watching for years, only lured back by the work of Hayao Miyazaki, who combined strong art with strong story.

STAGE 1: ADVENTURES IN ROCKETRY AND MEMORY

Okay, so you've watched *Spirited Away* and all the other Miyazaki movies you can get your hands on, and you look out at that vast sea of Japanese animation, and you suppose there must be something worth watching but you don't want to wade through the Sturgeon Ratio in order to find the rare gold. Good news: I will share my notes with you on *Wings of Honneamise,* "Voices of a Distant Star," *Millennium Actress,* and "Cowboy BeBop."

•

Royal Space Force: The Wings of Honneamise: (1987), 120 minutes. I first learned of *Wings of Honneamise* from Helen McCarthy's book *The Anime Movie Guide* (1996) wherein she has a "My Personal Top Ten" list, with Miyazaki movies taking positions one through four. *Wings of Honneamise* clocks in at number five. McCarthy writes of it:

> Real science fiction, world-building worthy to stand beside Miyazaki's, and a great story. In my opinion this is one of the best SF films ever made. Its slow pace, length and extended thematic development make demands on the audience which few Western

5

directors would risk, but it succeeds magnificently. (28)

I was skeptical of this high praise until I saw the movie, whereupon I find I agree with her in all points: it is hard SF anime, and as such exists in a class by itself.

The setting is a world with a 1950s level of technology (jet fighters, black and white television) and several different aristocratic governments. The opening monologue of the hero ends this way:

> When I was a kid, I wanted to be a Navy pilot. You had to join the Navy if you wanted to fly jets. They were so fast [. . .] Flew so high [. . .] For me there could be nothing better than flying. But, two months before I was to graduate from school, I saw that my grades weren't going to let me do any of that. And so [. . .] I ended up joining the Space Force.

Thus, from the get go, the Royal Space Force is revealed to be a joke, a collection zone for losers and dreamers. But they struggle through and build their rockets, which look like blends of early NASA and Soviet vehicles. It is sort of like imagining Jules Verne's gentlemen scientists working with only an "October Sky" shoestring budget and coming up with a rocket that might put a man into orbit.

The animation style is a little rough, especially if you've just come off a Miyazaki jag, but it is used very well. The faces of characters are not the typical anime style (i.e., big eyes; small mouths; sharp features), in fact they look potato-ish, lumpy and dull, and this is a refreshing difference from the standard fare. Most surprising to me, however, is the way that they have captured the "Miyazaki stillness" which is not as easy as it looks. This contributes to the "slow pace" that McCarthy notes.

The movie is also noteworthy for how it handles (an

invented) organized religion: the spiritual belief system is neither denigrated as nonsense nor lifted into the realm of woo-woo.

Wings of Honneamise is not for kids! There is an attempted rape scene. You have been warned.

•

"Voices of a Distant Star" (2003), 30 minutes. Directed by Makoto Shinkai. This film is boggling for two reasons. On the technical side, it is stunning because it was done by one man on a Macintosh computer, yet it does not look like "computer generated animation" as we have come to expect — it looks like beautiful, two-dimensional, traditional-style animation.

On the other side, I'm recommending a mecha movie here because it is really that good!

"Voices of a Distant Star" begins on Earth, in the middle of a campaign against alien invaders who blew up the domes on Mars. The characters are a middle-school boy and girl who are friends, shyly boyfriend and girlfriend, only she has been selected to be a mecha pilot and must leave Earth to fight for humanity. As she travels around at relativistic speeds the timelag between the couple increases. She goes through the trauma of the initial months of separation (and boot camp and combat) while he goes through the dull ache of years on Earth without her.

I have probably said too much already — it is only 30 minutes long!

Because it is one of the few anime to deal with relativistic time lag (yes, anime fans, it is like the 3.5-hours-long OVA series "GunBuster" [1988–89], but distilled and sharpened) I think of it as being true SF anime, giving *Wings of Honneamise* some much-needed company.

As a side note, this is one very rare case where I think that the English dub version is actually a little better than the Japanese version.

The DVD also comes with Shinkai's first film, "She and Her Cat" (2002), a 5 minute wonder that is devastatingly beautiful. I recommend it very highly. It is in black and white. It is about a young woman who has a cat. I really cannot say any more. Go ahead, watch it five times in a row — I did. (Tip of the hat to Adam Stephanides, who recommended "Voices of a Distant Star" to me based upon my quixotic quest for "true SF anime.")

•

Millennium Actress (2001; out on DVD in 2003), feature directed by Satoshi Kon. 1.5 hours. Set in Japan in 2001, a two-man documentary team is interviewing the elderly Chiyoko Fujiwara, a formerly great actress who has been in reclusive hiding for 30 years. What follows is a masterpiece of interwoven tales, where fact, fiction, and film blend and merge and cross-pollinate. Ah, but is it SF, you ask? This may be the first "New Wave Fabulist" movie ever made.

•

"Cowboy BeBop" Japanese TV series (1998–99), in six DVD volumes. Volume 1 has episodes 1 to 5, each one around 25 minutes long. There are 26 episodes, in total about 11 hours of viewing pleasure. First of all, I want to make it plain that I am not recommending *Cowboy BeBop: the Movie* because I found it to be a deep disappointment (almost as big a failure in going from the small screen to the big screen as *The Powerpuff Girl Movie* was).

I am recommending the TV series. And what a series it is!

Stunning soundtrack. Boggling animation. Exciting action. Funny scenes. It is like eating potato chips.

"Cowboy" is the future-slang term for bounty hunter; and the "BeBop" is a spaceship that flits around in the

Solar System, mainly around Mars and the asteroid belt, with occasional trips to Venus, battered Earth, and the Jovian moons. Initially the *BeBop* is crewed by Spike (the hero of the show, a man with a shady past) and Jet (an ex-cop who owns the ship).

The show reminds me favorably of anime's suave hero "Lupin III." Spike has a lot of the uncanny dexterity and nimble clowning that is the trademark of master thief Lupin, and the team of specialists that accumulates around him is similar to Lupin's cast of friendly foes and sidekicks. But Spike is not just a Lupin clone — there is a dark side that is explored in the larger story arc.

"Cowboy BeBop" is a cool, jazzy, grungy, retro kind of SF adventure. I am reminded of fiction by Alfred Bester, William Burroughs, and Samuel R. Delany. ("Big Shot," the bounty hunter infotainment TV show-within-the-show reminds me of fictional "The Tenth Victim" crossed with real-life "America's Most Wanted.") There are some hard SF details: there is no obvious artificial gravity (ships and stations use spinning habitat rings to create simulated gravity in many cases), there are no laser pistols (instead they use recognizable 20th century firearms that still use brass casings rather than more skiffy caseless ammo), and there is a faster-than-light "stargate" type of system for use within the Solar System, in tacit recognition of the transit times for ships travelling between the planets. (There are plenty of science-detail failures, but this seems typical in Sci Fi anime, so I applaud the successes where I can.)

The episodes range from great to only okay; the overall story arc is very good. I think the first disc is solid, the second disc is the weakest. In addition to the full set of six discs there is a "best of" disc that has six episodes: #1 "Asteroid Blues," #5 "Ballad of Fallen Angels," #19 "Wild Horses" [sic], #8 "Waltz for Venus," #17 "Mushroom Samba," and #24 "Hard Luck Woman." (Personally I think four of them are among the best but I don't rank #19 or #8 as being so high — I would replace them with #11 "Toys in the Attic," and either #2 "Stray Dog Strut,"#15 "My Funny Valentine," or #22 "Cowboy Funk.")

•

I have just recommended 15 hours worth of anime! Some of these titles may be hard to find, but I am pleased to put in a plug for Netflix, the DVD-rental-by-mail subscription service, which is where I rented all of the above except for *Wings of Honneamise*.

•

References

McCarthy, Helen. *The Anime Movie Guide*. The Overlook Press: Woodstock, 1996.

STAGE 2: EXPLORING ALIEN CHILDHOOD

This time I am recommending four titles from Japanese television: "FLCL," "NieA under Seven," "Haibane Renmei," and "Boogiepop Phantom: Evolution."

The episodes in these series are 22 minutes long. They are not "stand alone episodes;" they are chapters in a narrative.

Each series has an "age code" rating, similar to the American movie codes (G, PG-13, R, and X) in theory but not exactly the same: they are along the lines of "suggested 15+" which means "recommended for viewers aged 15 years and older."

•

"FLCL" (2000), science fiction/action/comedy from Gainax (the studio that made *Wings of Honneamise*). Six episodes on three discs (three hours total). Suggested for ages 15 and up: "MTV style" brief nudity, sexual humor, mild profanity, sexual innuendo, violence, and underage tobacco use.

Gender watch: this is a boy show.

"FLCL" (pronounced "fooley coolly") is centered upon Naota, a 12 year-old boy living in a small town in Japan with his failed-artist father and grumpy grandpa, while his big brother Tasuku is away playing baseball in America. Nothing ever happens in his town . . . there is a brand new factory, a post-modern whimsy that looks like a giant clothes iron, but nobody seems to work there and nothing seems to be produced.

We quickly come to see that Naota is having difficulty growing up in the shadow of his big brother, and/or coping with his absence. In the latter case, he is not alone, since high school girl Mamimi misses Tasuku so much she hangs out with Naota, whom she calls "Takkun" (a pet form of "Tasuku"). She kisses him frequently and gives him hickies. His friends are enviously scandalized and call the 17-year-old dropout his wife.

On the bridge where Mamimi hangs out, Naota is struggling to voice some terrible secrets to her, something about a recent letter from his brother, and maybe also his own love for her, which is tangled up with fear that he is only a Tasuku-surrogate for her.

The clouds gather behind him as he starts to speak, but suddenly a 19-year-old woman named Haruko blows into town on a Vespa motor scooter, wielding a gasoline-powered bass guitar like a battle-axe. She lays Naota out cold and when he wakes up there is a horn growing out of his forehead where the bass hit him.

That's the first four minutes or so. Then the horn grows and a big creature comes out of it. But Naota keeps assuring us that nothing ever happens in his town.

Powered by a driving rock soundtrack (from power-trio group "the Pillows," who are "the Pixies" of Japan), "FLCL" is fast, funny, and full of surprises. It is a surreal invasion of the mundane; the mundane absorption of the surreal. It is metaphor made concrete, as these artifacts spring Athena-like from the boy's head. It is whimsical and funny as well as seething with the dark Freudian world à la David Lynch, a nightscape where Oedipus and Cronos battle it out for the favors of Salome. It hits the system like a sugar-rush, or a double-espresso. It is the thunder of

Jupiter, the laughter of lightning.

•

"NieA under Seven" (2000). Drama/Comedy in 13 episodes on four discs (6.5 hours total), for ages 13 and up: mild profanity, violence. (Sometimes written as "NieA_7.")

Gender watch: ostensibly a girl show because it features a suffering heroine, it seems to be gender neutral.

If "FLCL" is a rocket trip, then *NieA* is a seesaw ride of alternating slapstick and heartache.

Contrary to expectations, the central figure is not NieA; it is her roommate Mayuko, a starving student working several part-time jobs and living in a room above a public bathhouse. Their situation is similar to that found in *The Odd Couple*, where Mayuko is hard working and NieA is profoundly lazy.

NieA is an alien from another star system—the mother ship crashed years ago and it is visible on the horizon, a flying saucer with a curled antenna. The aliens in Japan, refugees from the crash, nearly all have antennae on their heads. Each alien tends to imitate a human culture in a superficial way, so there is an alien-Chinese (she dresses in Chinese clothes and spouts Maoist proclamations), an alien-Hindu, and an alien-Hawaiian, among others.

There is a social ranking system used by the aliens, the higher the number the better, but the ranking also extends into negative territory, the so-called "unders." Which is the level where we find NieA, whose surname is "under seven" (i.e., "social rank minus seven," which appears to be the lowest possible ranking). NieA has no antenna and so she could pass for human (except for her elfin ears). (This "under" business sounds like Cordwainer Smith's "underpeople," but it is not really that way.)

Most of the aliens are striving to increase their rank by taking jobs, even menial jobs, to better themselves. NieA does not give a fig and refuses to work. She is a freeloader on Mayuko. Her only activity is to build mini flying saucers out of parts she has scrounged from the dump, but she makes these things in the single room of Mayuko's tiny apartment where they take up too much space.

How does Mayuko endure this? She is normally calm, sweet, and self-effacing, but NieA's freeloading behavior drives her to violent outbursts. At school Mayuko has to interact with spoiled students who are neither starving nor studying—parent-supported party girls who throw money around while Mayuko calculates whether she can afford to buy a can of cola. She is being squished from above (party girls) as well as from below (NieA).

But there is also the mystery of her past. Mayuko's family once owned the bathhouse where now she is a boarder who works in lieu of rent. Her father died some time ago and she is still coming to grips with this loss. In this way she is haunted and even something of a gothic heroine, living on as a lowly servant in the ruins of her ancestral castle.

NieA's antics and the fights she gets into with Mayuko provide the comedy, which in turn is tempered by the heartache of Mayuko's veiled past and her uphill struggle for a better future.

•

"Haibane Renmei" (2002). Drama: 13 episodes on four discs (6.5 hours total). For ages 13 and up: tobacco use, somber themes of life and death. Available on Netflix.

Gender watch: neutral/girl, or slightly more girlish than NieA yet still not an unmistakable "girl show."

This series is recommended for people who like John Crowley's fiction: a wonderful fairy-realism of poignant sweetness and light, against which rises a tide of dark melancholy.

The central character of "Haibane Renmei" is a teenage

girl called Rakka. In the opening scene she seems to fall through the sky, then we find her gestating within a plant that has sprouted like a weed inside an abandoned room of a large, old building. Several teenage girls with floating halos and small wings attend Rakka's subsequent birth as a teen from this plant. They look like angels but they are called "haibane" (which means "gray feathers"), and each emerged from a plant just as Rakka did. After a while Rakka goes through pain as her wings erupt from her back, and she is given her freshly minted halo—she is a haibane.

Rakka's group of haibane lives in "Old Home," an abandoned building on the outskirts of town. The haibane serve the humans of the town, each according to his or her ability: one works at a bakery, one works at a library, etc. The town is European in design and relatively low tech— the sort of "soft 1930s" technology level one associates with Miyazaki's movies. But the town is surrounded by a wall that seems at least a thousand feet tall, signifying that access from the outside world is strictly controlled and egress by the haibane is forbidden.

It is a sweet town full of fairly nice people, and the communal life of "Old Home" seems pleasant, but as Rakka learns more about this strange new world, she discovers some disturbing facts. A lot of the sadness comes to focus on Rakka's sister-haibane, Reki—the one who wears a leather jacket and smokes cigarettes. It turns out that not all haibane are equal when they come out of the cocoon: a rare few are "sin bound," and their feathers are black instead of ash-colored. This condition is due to actions in their lives before they came out of the cocoon.

"Haibane Renmei" is a sweet yet aching tale of self-discovery in a purgatorial landscape. The haibane have halos and small wings but they have no special powers (they cannot even fly). They manufacture their own halos in a technological way. The "haibane renmei" is the Haibane Association, the religious, aloof group that controls the haibane as well as the strange caravans that come into the town from the outside world.

•

"Boogiepop Phantom: Evolution" (2001), horror. Twelve episodes on four discs (4.4 hours total), for ages 15 and up: violence, drug use, and sexual situations.

Gender watch: this is horror, which is neutral/boy, I guess.

Where "Haibane Renmei" shows an otherworldly purgatory, "Boogiepop Phantom" reveals a spooky hell on Earth. The title sounds ridiculous at first, but there is a character named "Boogiepop," so it is not nonsensical.

The opening is not at all inspiring: a boogie pop tune accompanies a montage of grainy, live-action urban scenes. Some animated glowing butterflies flutter about. A young woman wearing a tall hat and a long billowing cloak appears: she is presumably Boogiepop, since one sees her on the DVD case and the disc itself.

Now something interesting happens: a series of three character cameos, giving their character names, as if this were a live-action drama of earlier decades. First is Toka, a girl in a high school uniform. Next is the tough and beautiful Nagi, clad in a leather racing-suit, looking out over the nighttime city astride her motorcycle (she is a ghost fighter). Third is Mr. Kuroda, a detective. We assume these three to be central characters, a team against the forces of darkness: perhaps Nagi is the heroine and the other two are her assistants . . .

Not exactly.

The series begins with an event that lasts one minute. Something violent happens on the roof of Shinyo Academy in the middle of the night: there is a scream; a spray of blood against the water tower; a silent blast that bends the metal railing and sends a shower of shattered glass falling into the swimming pool; a pillar of light that goes up into the sky; a shockwave that rolls through the city and triggers a momentary power outage. This is the "Manticore" event, and it will turn out to be one of the central mysteries of the series.

"Boogiepop Phantom" is like a cross between David Lynch's "Twin Peaks" and Kurosawa's *Rashomon*. There is a huge cast and the big story is revealed through the little horror stories of minor characters who are all high school students: we do not actually see much of Toka, Nagi, or Mr. Kuroda, yet they are pivotal characters. This is a challenge for the viewer.

The first episode is about Moto, a sophomore at Hijiridani High School. She has secretly been in love with the boy Saotome since junior high, when he was her best friend Yasuko's first sexual boyfriend until Yasuko dumped him. But Saotome disappeared on "the night of the light" (the Manticore event): some students think he was taken by Death, others think he was taken by "Boogiepop," a sinister figure of their own urban legends. Yasuko, now promiscuous, drags Moto out to a karaoke party, and on the way back Moto sees Saotome's ghost in an alley. Moto screams, but she will not tell what she saw.

On the schoolyard the next day, Yasuko tells Moto that Saotome's heart was recently broken by an older girl named Nagi.

"I once thought I was the reason he disappeared," says Yasuko. "But I guess I'm not."

Searching for the hidden thread of Saotome's life, Moto goes to the Shinyo Academy to find Nagi (who is a senior there), but she briefly meets Toka instead and learns that Nagi has a strange reputation. Unable to meet Nagi, Moto pushes onward by herself and comes face to face with the ghost . . .

The series is not entirely linear. The first few episodes are set about a month after the Manticore event. The fourth episode jumps back to an earlier point in time. One often sees the same scene from a different perspective. So the series is challenging in this way, too.

On the production side, "Boogiepop Phantom" is a technical marvel, a tour de force. The animation initially seems just average, but it has been tricked out in several ways: the color palette is one of muted tones; there is a fuzzy darkness to the screen edge; and the use of darkness and stillness is masterful. All this would be nothing if it were not supported by the most impressive use of sound in any animation I have seen: the ambient sound, the music, the sound effects all combine to form a sonic landscape of dread and suspense. When a monster talks, the reverse-reverb sound is quite spooky.

Everything is in a state of flux. Few things are what they seem to be. After watching a few episodes one learns to see the goofy glowing butterflies of the opening introduction as portents of terror.

Here I am recommending a series about a teenage investigator of the paranormal! That in itself is a testament to how good I think it is.

•

Childhood: Discarded, Missing, and Buried

The loss of childhood is an element common to these four television shows.

In "FLCL" the point is made that lying to others is adult behavior while lying to oneself is childish. This seems slightly twisted at first but then it becomes clear that Naota's problems come from his lying to himself, from acting "older" than he really is: he is made a "fool" by pretending to be so "cool." He has discarded his childhood in his anxious race to grow up.

With Mayuko and NieA in "NieA under Seven" we have two sides of a different coin: Mayuko seems to be missing or suppressing memories of her childhood beyond the age of seven or so (a time when her father was still alive) whereas NieA refuses to "grow up" into a responsible adult. This symmetry causes me to wonder if NieA is really an alternate persona of Mayuko: either she is an "imaginary friend" or a Mr. Hyde to Mayuko's Dr. Jekyll. There are definitely points in the show where NieA might be construed as being "imaginary" (there are a few times when Mayuko asks the bathhouse's furnace man if he has seen NieA around and he gets a blank look for a moment or two, saying "NieA?" as if he had never met her). There are even points that make one question whether NieA is really an alien or not (her lack of an antenna causes abusive comments from other aliens). Pursuing this thread, I wonder if the whole social ranking system is just a mask for the childhood age "under seven": that is, there is evidence that Mayuko's father died and the family was uprooted when she was "under seven" years of age. These are my musings: the show gives no solid answers, but plenty of tantalizing clues.

As for the haibane of "Haibane Renmei," when these angel-like beings emerge from their plant-wombs they have amnesia about their life before. The first memory they have is their cocoon-dream, which forms the basis of their new name as haibane ("rakka" means "to fall," from Rakka's dream of falling through the sky; "reki" means "pebbles" from the path in Reki's dream). The dream may be related to the dreamer's previous life; the inability to remember the entire dream may be what separates the sin-bound haibane from the majority; so the sin-bound are stigmatized by their pre-haibane lives.

Most haibane seem to be at peace with their previous lives, in the same way that a well-adjusted adult is at peace with her previous stages of childhood and teen years. The sin-bound haibane seem to be confronted with an "undigested past" that they must work through, like amnesia-sufferers piecing together painful traumas.

"Boogiepop Phantom" is a high school bloodbath. Childhoods are discarded, stolen, substituted, mutilated. But for these students the children's world of fairytales and theme parks is as much of a trap as the adult world of sex and intoxication. There are no easy answers and Death looms everywhere.

These four shows reveal different approaches to the loss of childhood. Naota, who had discarded his childhood, is able to reclaim it while still a child; Mayuko, whose childhood is missing, feels herself slowly coming to recognize and accept those early traumas; Rakka, whose previous life has been encoded as a dream, struggles to unearth what has been buried; the characters of "Boogiepop Phantom" struggle in the dark maze and many die.

•

The manic "FLCL," the manic-depressive "NieA under Seven," the sweetly depressive "Haibane Renmei," and the genuinely spooky "Boogiepop Phantom: Evolution": each one stands out from the typical "Sci Fi anime" crowd; each offers an SF vision, albeit not one of "hard SF," but "true SF" nonetheless.

STAGE 3: LEAPS IN SPACE & TIME

At long last, two science fiction items to write home about: "Planetes" (a TV series available in the US on DVD) and *The Girl Who Leapt Through Time* (a feature film).

•

"Planetes" (2003–04, US 2005–06) is that very rare item, a "hard SF" anime. It is a 26 episode TV series, with each episode being 25 minutes long. It is in the tradition of *Wings of Honneamise* (1987), the only other member of this category (note the 16-year gap). The production value is good but not groundbreaking, having some of the look and feel of Satoshi Kon's "Magnetic Rose," a section of the anthology *Memories* (1995). This is not "space opera," with larger-than-life characters battling it out for the fate of the galaxy, this is "hard life for the manual laborer" in a de-glamorized Earth space environment of A.D. 2075, where orbiting space junk has become a navigational hazard that must be removed. This is a show about garbage men in space.

The collectors of orbital debris face occupational hazards and the difficulties of low social status. One immediately senses that ISPV 7, the space station they work out of, is overstaffed at the upper echelons — it is top-heavy, with too many managers and not enough workers. Debris Section has a total staff of seven people. The "garbage truck" vehicle itself usually has four people in it — the 20-something hero, a Japanese guy called "Hachimaki" who is trying to get the work done, a female American pilot named Fee, a Russian guy named Yuri, and the newbie, a Japanese woman named Ai Tanabe who serves as the entry point character. These four are the ones out there risking their lives in space walks and demolitions.

Back at the office there are three more characters — a bumbling section boss, a goofy Indian guy always practicing his magic tricks, and a super-efficient temp worker. This setting provides humor and complications, a light version of British TV show "The Office." Further up the chain is the station's Control Section, which adds a bit of British TV show "Upstairs, Downstairs" to the mix — Hachimachi's ex-girlfriend Claire is an upstairs clerk serving in the quasi-military environment of handling mission control and traffic control, a place similar to a starship's bridge.

As the series begins, Hachimaki's job satisfaction has declined almost to the point of burnout. Newbie Ai Tanabe's wide-eyed enthusiasm brings up his own bitterness and resentments, which forces him to confront his old dream of having a spaceship of his own — a dream that is slipping further away as his job becomes more of a dead end.

The hazards faced by the collectors range from immediate ones (like suit rips and equipment failure) to long term ones (radiation exposure, loss of bone mass, as well as mental diseases related to life in space). The show is not an unbearable downer, though, since there are jokes and camaraderie going on, in addition to the challenge of special missions. This was a shrewd move for the anime makers, allowing them to humanize a "realistic space" scenario that might otherwise be too depressing.

Plot-wise, the early episodes are not quite as snappy as the bounty hunter scenarios of "Cowboy BeBop." They have a good way of setting up tension, but sometimes the resolution/solution seems drawn out and slow to me. Some of this has to do with a warming up period, a certain easing of the viewer into the "hard SF" universe. Ai Tanabe is a bit shrill with her newbie-idealism and takes it pretty hard when things don't conform to it. This aspect seems to bother a number of American viewers, but most will acknowledge that she "gets better" as she learns. While I myself wasn't irritated by Ai's outbursts, I will admit that I found episode 6 (involving a group of ninja fans living their fantasy on the Moon) to be so light-hearted and silly that I worried the show might have already jumped the shark. My fears proved to be groundless, however, and judging the series as a whole, the structure of the beginning seems to be a necessary lightening up of a story that becomes darker and heavier as it progresses. Without giving too much of the story away, a large spaceship is being built in orbit for the first manned mission to Jupiter, and Hachimaki enters the trials to get a position onboard, but meanwhile terrorists from Earth feel the money would be better spent on improving the lot of their impoverished Third World countries. There are twists and turns to the story, with plenty of character development and increasing tension to a gripping climax, so the complete story arc is actually more satisfying than the complete "Cowboy BeBop" story.

The age rating for "Planetes" is 13+. It comes on six DVDs with five bonus discs.

•

The Girl Who Leapt Through Time (2006) is an animated feature (100 minutes) that has won several awards in Japan, but in the US it only was screened at a few film festivals. It is about Makoto, a high school girl who, yes, learns to travel back in time by way of a running long jump.

I've seen my share of time travel movies, from underrated gems like *La Jeteé* (1962) through popular films like *Groundhog Day* (1993) to the flawed *Butterfly Effect* (2004). As a result I've become very jaded about this subgenre, and yet *The Girl Who Leapt* somehow brings a fresh and lively example.

The Girl Who Leapt has a great look and feel, like a lower budget version of Satoshi Kon's *Millennium Actress* that compensates with higher energy levels. (Another reason it reminds me of *Millennium Actress* is the way that the heroine has several key running sequences.) The movie starts on an empty baseball diamond where Makoto is tossing the ball with her two friends, both boys. That's Makoto, a tomboy making wisecracks while she pitches the ball with casual expertise. She looks like a Miyazaki heroine with her short dark hair, but later on when you see her cry she shows such intensity that one reassesses Miyazaki's heroines as little soldiers who stoically knuckle away their one or two tears.

The Girl Who Leapt has a solid SF text pedigree, being based on a young adult novel by Yasutaka Tsutsui, one of the most famous Japanese SF authors. Initially published in serial form (1965–66), it was made into a live action TV series in 1972, and live-action movies in 1983 and 1997. This movie is not exactly a remake, though — it is an updating that makes it a kind of sequel, in that the heroine of the original story is Makoto's aunt.

Makoto goes through a spectrum of emotions in the course of the movie, which makes it a real emotional rollercoaster for the viewer. Once she discovers her power, she experiments with it to learn more, which leads to comedy, but as she learns her limits there is tension, the threat of tragedy, and a haunted quality. Part of it is that she is happy in her life as a student with two friends who are boys, and she doesn't want it to change through graduation or romantic complications. At the root of it she wants things to stay the same, but of course they cannot.

She comes to realize how fragile and fleeting happiness is, how it can develop so slowly as to be almost unnoticed until it is snatched away by the changes of Time.

The talent of the production side is stellar. The director, Mamoru Hosoda, is the man originally slated to direct Ghibli Studio's movie, *Howl's Moving Castle*. The character designer is none other than Yoshiyuki Sadamoto, founding member of Gainax, the studio that made *Wings of Honneamise* and "FLCL." Brought together by Madhouse, the studio that produced Satoshi Kon's four films to date, including *Millennium Actress*. It is a winning combination.

STAGE 4: INNER SPACE AND HIDDEN SPACE

Reviews of "Mushi-shi," *Paprika, The Place Promised in Our Early Days,* and "The Melancholy of Haruhi Suzumiya."

•

Review of anime series "Mushi-shi"

Miyazaki meets Lovecraft — it sounds impossible, or perhaps a joke like the short film "Bambi Meets Godzilla" (1969), but this twenty-six episode anime series delivers something unique, a blend of Miyazaki's beautiful nature scenery and Lovecraft's haunting dread of microbial eldritch entities. Imagine a mashup of the sunny village in *My Neighbor Totoro* (1988) with the spooky village of "The Dunwich Horror" (1929); or perhaps a fusion of the ecology in *Princess Mononoke* (1997) and the alien parasitism in "From Beyond" (1934).

Ginko the hero is a "mushi-shi," an investigator of supernatural entities called "mushi." Invisible to most people, mushi are strange creatures that blur the solid boundaries between plant, animal, and insect. They live in a hidden ecology all around us, feeding off of geomantic rivers of light that flow unseen. Most of them are small, but they can be surprisingly large.

The series is something like a medical detective show. Ginko arrives at an isolated village where something weird has been going on. He examines the afflicted humans, studying their strange growths or magical powers; he examines the local terrain, the plants, the soil, et cetera; and then he attempts a cure. Ginko himself is a white-haired man in his late 20s/early 30s. He has only one eye, the other having been lost under strange circumstances that are eventually revealed. The fact that he is a mysterious stranger with one eye who wanders around helping people with their supernatural problems makes him a bit of an Odin figure. But after a while one begins to wonder whose side he is on, meaning that he is less a "Shane" and more a Clint Eastwood or Indiana Jones. In Lovecraftian terms, such a character would be Herbert West, the re-animator. Ginko is something like a modern shaman, or an investigative alchemist — he is a master who knows his stuff, but he is always learning more, and we learn alongside him like an apprentice, seeing the new knowledge along with the depths of the old.

In Lovecraft's horror, any village is full of inhabitants who are clannish if not inbred, suspicious of strangers, and harboring dark secrets of local lore. This is basically how it is in "Mushi-shi," which is a far cry from the sunny villagers of Miyazaki's work.

Ginko's wardrobe is contemporary to the present day — he wears shirt, trousers, hiking shoes, and a trench coat when weather requires it. (The one odd thing is his backpack, which is a big wooden box with shoulder straps.) Yet the people he meets all wear kimono and Japanese footwear. There are no cars in evidence, no motorboats, no trains, and I don't recall seeing even a horse. Likewise there are no samurai or swords, no mention of shogun or emperor. People smoke tobacco, which historically began after a ban was lifted in the late 1600s; Ginko himself is always smoking cigarettes, which did not arrive in Japan until after 1868. It is a strangely timeless place, located somewhere between 1870 and 1890. Maybe. "Steampunk" without the steam, having instead an alien ecology, making it a Victorian nanobiotech punk. Perhaps.

The show opens with a tune in English, "The Sore Feet Song" by alternative music artist Ally Kerr. This is a simple composition of voice and acoustic guitar, a song one might hear performed in a coffeehouse or by a busker on the street, and as such it immediately gives a sense of both contemporary times and timelessness. The lyrics tell of the singer's travels across strange, exotic lands, searching for an unnamed person, place, or thing: "Through sandstorms and hazy dawns I reached for you." In Lovecraftian terms, this wandering minstrel's theme song matches "The Quest of Iranon" (1921) from the Dreamland Cycle, thus crystallizing the quintessence of "Mushi-shi."

Where "Mushi-shi" really hits the Lovecraft button is the way in which an entire mythos is presented over time, resulting in a system that is so original and non-derivative that it seems "true." The episodes are not gory horror, they are melancholic and haunting horror. Or creepy, in "the bug crawls in your ear and lays eggs" sort of way. Sometimes the episodes are like traditional Japanese ghost stories, reworked into a mushi mode; at other times they partake of myths from ancient Greece. Most of anime is highly derivative, which makes the whole-cloth originality of "Mushi-shi" all the more impressive.

"Mushi-shi" is based upon a manga of the same name, a series that spawned not only the TV show reviewed here but also a live action feature, *Bugmaster* (2006).

"Mushi-shi" (2005), by Funimation Productions (in North America). Six discs, a total of twenty-six episodes, each 25 minutes long. Rated TV-14 (viewers age fourteen and up). In Japanese and English-dub. Subtitles and bonus material, including interviews with the director and others. It is available for rental from Netflix.

Funimation has taken the brave step of having a

presence on YouTube, so you can watch English dub versions of several episodes right now, for free.

(I myself watched the subtitled version, for what it is worth.)

•

Review of Satoshi Kon's *Paprika*

Now available on DVD in North America, Satoshi Kon's latest film, *Paprika* (2006), is his most challenging work to date. It is about the DC-Mini, an experimental "dream machine" that allows a therapist to enter the dreams of her patient, and the potential for it to be misused as a weapon. Imagine an animated feature that is a reality-bending blend of Hitchcock's psychoanalytical thriller *Spellbound* (1945) and the cyberpunk movie *Strange Days* (1995), then crank it up. Because the film is so challenging, the following review will contain a lot of details that might seem like spoilers but in fact are merely enough to give readers the background and context to enjoy the movie in one viewing.

Paprika starts in the middle of a dream, where a detective is searching for a criminal at a circus. His partner seems to be a young female clown. Suddenly the circus magician performing in the center ring teleports the detective into a cage. Then the spectators in the bleachers all rush the cage, but they all have the detective's face. The ground gives way and the detective is falling through the air, but the young woman catches him while swinging by on a Tarzan vine. The pair races through several more movie scenes, chasing the fleeing criminal, before the detective wakes up in a panic.

He is in bed in a hotel room. In the other bed is the young woman with light brown hair. She is Paprika, his new therapist. Both patient and therapist wear on their respective heads a thing that looks like a cross between a hair comb and an earpiece: the DC-Mini.

They review the dream recorded on her laptop computer. Paprika is warm, playful, and coquettish, but when the session time is up she heads for the door. He is eager to see her again because she is literally the girl of his dreams. She leaves an appointment card for him.

She exits the building and rides away on a scooter, but as she rides through the opening credits she begins to change into a different woman, a cold adult with straight black hair. This is Dr. Atsuko Chiba.

Here is the background information. Dr. Chiba, 29 years old, is a highly placed research scientist at the Foundation for Psychiatric Research. A few years earlier, her colleague, the enormously fat Dr. Tokita, invented the DC-Mini. The Foundation created a new department to deal with the device, with Tokita to handle the hardware side and Chiba to oversee the clinical trials, which were limited to simply recording the dreams of mental patients.

However, Dr. Chiba could see that Dr. Tokita was having mental troubles of his own, and so they secretly experimented, breaking protocol by sharing a dream actively as a form of therapy. This experiment was where Chiba first adopted the persona of Paprika, the 18 year old girl, while sharing the dream space of another.

Tokita quickly got over his mental trouble, making the unauthorized experiment a success. Later on, their immediate boss Dr. Shima, a dwarfish man, began suffering from depression. So Paprika helped him, too, again resulting in rapid and successful healing. The third patient of this clandestine therapy is the detective, a friend of Dr. Shima from their college days. The detective is suffering from a recurring dream and the stress of a difficult murder case.

Got all that? Good. Because when Dr. Chiba gets back to her lab at the Foundation, fat Dr. Tokita tells her they have a crisis on their hands: three DC Minis have been stolen from his office. Drs. Chiba, Tokita, and dwarfish

Shima have an immediate meeting to figure out what to do in order to protect their project, but the Foundation's chairman, an elderly man in a wheelchair, interrupts them.

The chairman says he already knows about the security breach. He wants to shut down the DC-Mini project. He thinks the theft they have already suffered will lead to psychic-terrorism and he wonders if the rumored person "Paprika" is behind it. The pressure is on — not only is the project threatened, but so is Paprika herself.

Suddenly dwarfish Dr. Shima starts spouting nonsense, and he works himself into an enthusiasm that leads him to jump out the nearest window, high up in their multi-storied building. Luckily Shima survives his fall. They put him under observation, hooking him up to a DC-Mini, with the realization that they had witnessed the first "weaponized" use of the DC-Mini, exactly the sort of terrorism that the chairman had been talking about.

Watching the dream on the computer monitor, Dr. Chiba quickly sees that Shima has the dream of a mental patient planted in his brain. Tokita's theory is that Shima was monitoring a patient's dream during clinical trials when the terrorist used another DC-Mini to intrude, at which point the dream was projected into Shima's unconscious, where it was left like a remote-controlled bomb, waiting for the detonation signal to come. The sudden pressure of the crisis then triggered the unstable dream into taking over his waking consciousness.

Then the dream they are watching on the computer gives another clue, the appearance of fat Tokita's pudgy assistant Himuro, who spouts more of the same crazy talk that Shima had being saying during his episode. It turns out that Himuro hasn't been at the lab for a few days. He becomes the prime suspect of stealing the DC-Minis, and they go to his apartment to investigate.

There. That's the first fifteen minutes, with later details filled in for greater context. I've been careful not to ruin anything, but I'll go no further.

Fans of Kon's work know that he usually works with the breakdown of reality. In his films *Perfect Blue* (1997) and *Millennium Actress* (2001), the tension is between the everyday world and the world of film, and how they start to blend into each other. In his TV series "Paranoia Agent" (2004) the tension is between social reality and the social unreality expressed by such things as urban legends. Kon's *Tokyo Godfathers* (2003) is softer and more subtle, being ultimately a tension between the mundane and the miraculous, which makes it the best introduction to Kon's work.

With that said, *Paprika* presents the aforementioned breakdown taken to an even higher level, to the stage where dreams and reality blend and blur. This is the heady stuff of New Wave science fiction in its heyday, from A to Z: novels like Brian Aldiss's *Barefoot in the Head* (1969), where an LSD War has left the wounded walking in a stream-of-consciousness landscape, and especially Roger Zelazny's *Dream Master* (1966), about a therapist who uses a computer to enter/experience/shape the dreams of his patients. Although it seems to come straight from the New Wave, in fact *Paprika* is based upon a Japanese science fiction novel of the same name, published in 1993. Its author is Yasutaka Tsutsui, who has a long reputation as a "New Wave" writer in Japan (with a career spanning 1965 to the present), analogous to a Kurt Vonnegut or a Philip K. Dick, but he is virtually unknown elsewhere.

Given Kon's work, *Paprika* seems like a natural for him. It is, but in a far more complicated way than just that. For starters, Kon is a long-time fan of the novel *Paprika* and admits that most of his earlier work was inspired by it. Meanwhile, Tsutsui, having seen Kon's work, decided that Kon was the one to make a movie of *Paprika*. So this is one of those rare cases where the author starts the ball rolling, participates in a small role on screen (as a bartender), and sees it through to the end.

Fans of Kon's work will find much to love in *Paprika*, a

movie that starts with a bang and never lets up. Newcomers will be better prepared after reading this background information — looking over other reviews, it really bugs me that so many say that "a machine" has been stolen, when in crucial fact it is three machines that have been stolen. That seemingly innocuous simplification amounts to obfuscating misinformation.

While not for everyone, Kon's signature style of reality-breakdown is dizzying, dazzling, and delightful. Cinephiles especially are urged to give him a try.

Paprika (2006), Sony Pictures Classics. 86 minutes. Rated R (for violent and sexual images). In Japanese, English-dub, French-dub, and Spanish-dub. Subtitles and bonus material, including interviews with director Kon and author Tsutsui. It is available for rental from Netflix.

•

Review of Makoto Shinkai's *The Place Promised in Our Early Days*

Makoto Shinkai is being called the "new Miyazaki," and his first feature-length anime gives some traction to the claim.

The film is *The Place Promised in Our Early Days* (2004), which won two awards in Japan and has just been released on DVD in America. Only 90 minutes long, the story is set in northern Honshu, the main island of Japan, in an alternate history where the Soviets occupied Hokkaido, the northern island of Japan, at the end of World War II. It is 1996 and two boys in junior high are keenly interested in the enigmatic tower built by the "Union" in now-foreign Hokkaido. The world wonders if it is a scientific device, or a weapon, or perhaps both. The boys want to see it up close, but the border has been closed for decades, and so they work at building their own airplane to fly across the strait and back again.

The other shared interest the best friends have is Sayuri

Sawatari, a girl in their class. She slips into their confidence, learns about their secret project, and is so enthusiastic that they promise to take her along when they fly.

But then suddenly Sayuri moves away without a word. The boys, embittered, drift apart. Three years go by, and the desire for Japanese Reunification propels America and the Union toward a possibly apocalyptic war. One boy works in a government lab dedicated to solving the mystery of the tower, and he begins to use smuggled Union science; the other boy is haunted by the memory of the girl who disappeared from their lives, and the unfulfilled promise; while the girl herself is in a hospital, trapped in a quasi-dream state that is somehow linked to the tower's secret activation in 1996.

The Place Promised is Shinkai's third project. The first was "She and Her Cat" (1999), a five-minute, black and white animation that he made by himself on a Macintosh computer. The film, an intensely poignant tale of a single woman and her pet, won a few awards. Next came "Voices of a Distant Star" (2003), 25 minutes of vivid color animation about a schoolgirl who goes off to war among the stars and the effects of the email time lag on her boyfriend left behind. Again the animation was done entirely by Shinkai on a Mac, and in the DVD bonus interview he is clearly exhausted by it. *The Place Promised* is the first time he has used a real team.

Shinkai's work bears resemblance to that of Miyazaki at several points. The backgrounds are beautifully detailed, revealing the wondrous beauty in everything around us, from a field of grass on a summer's day to the play of reflected light on the ceiling of a moving train car. There is a strong emotional current connecting the landscape to the characters, creating a sense of how time and place and character all come together — a nostalgia for the real as well as a longing for places that never existed. Miyazaki and Shinkai also share a certain interest in unusual aircraft.

On the other hand, Miyazaki's bustling optimism and action orientation is quite different from Shinkai's haunting sadness and melancholic endurance.

Added to the pedigree of *The Place Promised* is a strong sense of that "hard SF" anime milestone, *Wings of Honneamise* (1987), the anime feature about a "royal space force" that goes from being a joke to launching their world's first manned rocket. Without giving away key plot points the two movies have, it is enough to say that every time a jet plane flew overhead in *The Place Promised* I was reminded of the opening scene of *Wings*; and whenever the boys worked on their airplane it was depicted with the same sort of loving detail and hobbyist energy found with the team of misfits building their rocket; and *Wings* also has a dollop of that haunting sadness. *Wings* was the first anime from Gainax, a company which has had a long string of successes since then, including the series "GunBuster" (1988–89) about a schoolgirl sent to war among the stars (the likely inspiration for Shinkai's "Voices of a Distant Star").

The Place Promised is a beautiful movie. Sentimental and multi-layered, it rewards multiple viewing but is not so complex that one cannot comprehend it on one viewing. It has a haunting sense of familiarity, which feeds into our own latent nostalgia for the Cold War era: the country is divided, as Germany once was and Korea remains, with reunification seeming almost certain to be apocalyptic; the tower is a souped-up cross between the Berlin Wall (an architectural monument built in 1961) and Sputnik (a scientific/military marvel launched in 1957); the plan of the boys to fly a home-built plane into forbidden territory recalls the time in 1987 when West German teenager Mathias Rust flew a small plane from Helsinki to Red Square in Moscow, through the tightest airspace in the world; the year 1999 reminds us of the millennialism, adding to the sense of potential apocalypse.

The Place Promised is rated 13+, which would be

something like "PG" or "PG-13" in the US: appropriate for viewers teenaged and older (some violence). It is available for rental from Netflix.

•

Review of anime series "The Melancholy of Haruhi Suzumiya"

"The Melancholy of Haruhi Suzumiya" is an animated TV series from Japan that became an Internet phenomenon, then a worldwide cult hit. Now it is available on American DVD.

The first episode features a curvaceous high school girl in a variety of sexy costumes (waitress and bunny girl) in an opening sequence artfully constructed to seem like the work of rank amateurs — the titling is awkward, the film editing is rough, the music sounds tinny, and the vocalist sounds as though she is singing a karaoke song for the first time. It looks like a student film project, something like an amateur *Barbarella*, that is an unintentional parody of teen-exploitation movies.

The story that follows is delightfully incoherent. It involves Mikuru, a "combat waitress" (!) sent from the future to secretly protect Koizumi, a high school boy who doesn't know about his own untapped psionic powers. As a part of her undercover role she has a day job as a shopping mall booster, during which she wears the bunny girl costume and waves signs to draw business to a number of small shops. (This is how they attempt to justify the use of the sexy costumes.) Her secret mission is to foil the villain Yuki, an evil sorceress from another planet who wants to subvert the boy for her own unfathomable alien purposes.

Kyon the cameraman provides the movie's deadpan narration, pointing out flaws in technique as well as the huge holes in the plot. It becomes clear that Kyon has feelings for Mikuru and wants to protect her from exploitation, even though he was the one who filmed her. That being the case, there seems to be some sort of coercion going on behind the scenes.

Things go wildly awry in the first combat between Mikuru and Yuki, and the schoolgirl director herself briefly enters the scene, shouting, "Cut!" and making a fuss. Then there is a commercial for a local electronics store featuring Mikuru in the bunny costume and Yuki holding the sign.

The movie downshifts into a high school love triangle, then morphs into a newlywed comedy, before finding its way to a climactic rooftop battle scene.

When the movie ends after about twenty minutes we see the cast and crew in a projection room where they have just previewed their project for the first time. The narrator Kyon is appalled by the poor quality of the movie, but the director is gushing with enthusiasm, and her name is Haruhi Suzumiya. This hints at the true structure of the series, in which Haruhi is the madcap star and Kyon is the deadpan straight man who is narrating directly to us.

The second episode is actually the one that comes first in chronological order (the series ping-pongs around in a nonlinear way — the first episode is chronologically the eleventh). It is the first day of high school and the new students are introducing themselves to their homeroom classmates. Haruhi stands up and says, "I have no interest in ordinary humans. If there are any aliens, time travelers, sliders, or psionic mutants here, come join me. That is all!"

The students and the teacher look at her in openmouthed shock.

This is Haruhi — beautiful, headstrong, eccentric, highly competitive, and highly competent. She is a mercurial dictator searching for something she can't quite name, and she quickly draws the four other characters of the series into orbiting around her. Each episode has Haruhi leading them through a different madcap adventure — playing in an amateur baseball league, trying to locate a missing student, beating the computer club president at his favorite video game, or making a movie for the school festival. Each time Kyon tries to talk her out of her new brainstorm, then tries to prevent exploitation of Mikuru, and usually fails at both. It might seem like the standard setup for a mundane high school comedy, yet there is a weirdness going on, even from the first episode, that clearly signals true science fictional content.

Involving aliens, time travelers, sliders, and psionic mutants.

In addition to dictator Haruhi and narrator Kyon, the main cast is rounded out with the three characters seen in the student movie of the first episode. Mikuru (who played the combat waitress) is an upperclassman selected by Haruhi precisely because she is super-cute and super-pliable. Koizumi (who played the boy unaware of his psionic powers) is a mysterious transfer student who acts as an enabler for Haruhi, much to Kyon's dismay. And Yuki (who played the alien magician) is a bookworm who says little and seems to go along with whatever Haruhi comes up with. Obviously Kyon has his hands full trying to keep things from spinning out of control.

The series has excellent production values. The animation itself is high quality, the writing is snappy, the music is great, and the strategy of making the series nonlinear turns out to be brilliant. There is an impressive balancing act between parody and originality, comedy and drama, with the wheels spinning within wheels throughout the show. The closing theme song is catchy enough to have become a pop hit in Japan and is boosted by animation showing the characters doing a very cute dance. This dance proved to be a big help in making the series an Internet sensation.

•

Television programming is not nearly as nationwide in

Japan as it is in America, and "The Melancholy of Haruhi Suzumiya" had a limited audience when the first episode aired in the Tokyo area on April 2, 2006. The audience fell in love with the show and that little dance at the end of each episode provided an immediate catalyst.

Brief clips started showing up on YouTube. At first they were just the ending theme song sequence from the show, and home videos of fans performing the dance either solo or in full five-member ensembles. Then there was a stop motion version of the dance using model robots from Gundam, a classic anime series. Parodies and homage burst forth. Fan activity was heating up and it suddenly became apparent that YouTube was very popular in Japan, even more popular than in America. "Haruhi Suzumiya" was an Internet sensation. By May there were videos of teams doing the dance on auditorium stages outside of Japan, in Taiwan and elsewhere. Full episodes were uploaded, with English subtitles provided by fans. It got to the point where the fan-subtitled episode was being uploaded only four days after the original broadcast, allowing YouTubers around the world to watch the Japanese TV series in something close to real time.

Increased interest led to wider broadcast in Japan. The show itself continued to deliver, never losing that initial sparkle. The last episode was aired on July 2. Two months later, *Newsweek* ran a story about the surprising popularity of YouTube in Japan, mentioning "Haruhi Suzumiya" by name. During that same month, sales figures confirmed the story — where a "smash hit" is defined as 10,000 discs sold, Episode 00 sold 70,000 discs and DVD 1 sold 90,000 discs.

And now the show is coming to America, only 13 months after premiering in Japan.

•

After all my praise for the nonlinear aspect of the

show, the DVDs themselves provide some complications — DVD 1 begins with episode eleven (the student film) but then proceeds in strictly chronological order from episode one. I think this is an outrage. I have nothing against watching the series in chronological order, but I think it is best done as a second viewing rather than as a first viewing. (The broadcast order is more satisfying because the excitement of chronological episodes five and six provides a thunderous ending to the series.) Fortunately the broadcast order is available on three bonus discs, starting with the Special Limited Edition DVD 2 (the first disc has the first five episodes). While this is the best way to see the show, the Special Limited Edition is more expensive than the standard edition.

Netflix is not carrying the bonus discs at the time of this writing, and I suspect that other rental outlets will be the same, so here is a plan to trick out a broadcast order from the standard DVDs — rent DVD 1 and DVD 2; watch the first three episodes on DVD 1 (eleven, one, and two); watch episode seven on DVD 2; finally go back to DVD 1 and watch episode three. This puts a third of the series in the right order. It lacks only the funny "Next Episode" segments, in which Kyon and Haruhi argue about the numbering, but that is relatively minor.

Here is a table to help make sense of it all.

Broad. Episode	Title	Chron. Episode	DVD Disc
1	Adventures of Mikuru	11	1
2	Melancholy . . . Pt. 1	1	1
3	Melancholy . . . Pt. 2	2	1
4	Boredom	7	2
5	Melancholy . . . Pt. 3	3	1
6	Remote . . . Pt. 1	9	3
7	Mysterique Sign	8	3
8	Remote . . . Pt. 2	10	3
9	Someday in the Rain	14	4
10	Melancholy . . . Pt. 4	4	2
11	Day of Sagittarius	13	4
12	Live Alive	12	4
13	Melancholy . . . Pt. 5	5	2
14	Melancholy . . . Pt. 6	6	2

Even science fiction fans who don't usually watch anime will get a big kick out of "The Melancholy of Haruhi Suzumiya," a science fiction high school high jinks romantic comedy. There are fourteen episodes, each one twenty-four minutes long, for a total of 5.6 hours of entertainment. The show rewards multiple viewing, but such is not required. (Once you know that a certain character really is an extraterrestrial android, then her previous statements turn out to be more revealing the second time around.) It is rated the equivalent of PG-13 since some of the teen-exploitation is inappropriate for younger viewers.

ESCAPE VELOCITY: TELEMETRY

Notes on "Haibane Renmei" (apparent influences upon the series) and "Planetes" (contrasting the manga and the anime).

•

Apparent Influences in "Haibane Renmei"

The anime TV series "Haibane Renmei" (2002) has at least four inspirations: the personal sorrow of creator Yoshitoshi ABe; the art genre of "bad girl" angel posters sold in the 1990s; the 12-minute American indy film "This Guy Is Falling" (2000); and a couple of novels by Japanese author Haruki Murakami.

The sorrow of ABe is the most important, but also the most obscure, as his autobiographical statements on the subject have been very few. In a video interview in 2003, ABe said of "Haibane Renmei,"

> "I wanted to write a story based on the period starting from when I had been suffering to the point when I had felt like I'd found salvation. My experience is filtered into a fictional story, but if I could have the audience feel something similar to what I had felt in the end [then I would achieve my

goal]." (5:14)

Earlier in the same interview (bonus material on "Haibane Renmei" DVD 4) he indicated that this period was "ten or eleven years" in the past (4:09). Since the interview took place in 2003, this implies that ABe's sorrow was in 1992 or 1993, when ABe was 21 or 22 years old. Then again, the ten years might relate to when he started writing the story rather than the year of the interview: the first version was published in 1998, and the second version, much closer to the anime, came out in 2001. The earlier date pushes ABe's sorrow back to 1987, when he was 16 years old, which has a strong connection to the similarly youthful heroine of "Haibane Renmei."

Beyond these few facts regarding ABe's sorrow, there is only speculation. The story of "Haibane Renmei" suggests that ABe had a close friend, perhaps a girlfriend, who committed suicide despite his best efforts to help. According to this line of interpretation, ABe might be represented in the anime as the crow at the very beginning, and later as the crow's skeleton in the dry well of episode 8. But this is only speculation.

As for "bad girl" angels, I recall seeing many ads for such posters as I flipped through the pages of glossy magazines like *Science Fiction Age* in the '90s. It seemed like a genre unto itself: teen angels smoking cigarettes, wearing leather jackets, et cetera. True, in "Haibane Renmei" there are a lot of girl angels, and only a couple of them are "bad girls," but those two are very important.

If that is too easy a catch, the short film "This Guy Is Falling" (directed by Michael Horowitz and Gareth Smith) is not. In this case I am fairly convinced that "Haibane Renmei"'s opening imagery and theme song ("Free Bird") come from the opening imagery and music of "This Guy Is Falling" (hereafter "TGIF"). TGIF opens with a tracking shot, down from the sky through the clouds to the city below, which I'll grant is fairly generic; "Haibane

Renmei" makes it more gripping by showing a young woman falling through the sky. (For what it is worth, TGIF is an action comedy that involves people later falling through the sky.) But the music sounds very similar to me, in tune and instrumentation, and TGIF came first. TGIF uses the same music in longer form near the end, starting at around 9:20.

The Murakami connection to "Haibane Renmei" is fairly well established. Viewers noticed the connection between "Haibane Renmei"'s walled town of Glie and the weird walled town "The End of the World" in Murakami's two-track novel *Hard-Boiled Wonderland and the End of the World* (1985). The novel even has a map of the town in the frontispiece, showing the encircling wall, the clock tower, the river, the various named woods, and the library, all features shared with Glie. "The End of the World" track of the novel has a main character who lacks memory of his previous life, an amnesia which is lifted through stages, a pattern very much like the situation in "Haibane Renmei." Things diverge a bit: Murakami's Library has unicorn skulls that the hero learns to read; ABe's Library has a "fossilized" book. Murakami's town is more weird and spooky; ABe's Glie seems to draw from the anime of Miyazaki's fantasy type of idealized European town, with cute cafes, wholesome bakeries, modern wind turbines generating electricity, medieval clock towers undergoing repair, and Vespas whirring down cobblestone streets. That is, ABe's town is like a place in Miyazaki's *Kiki's Delivery Service* (1989) or *Porco Rosso* (1992).

The dry well featured so dramatically in "Haibane Renmei" episodes 8 and 9 comes straight from a different Murakami book, *The Wind-up Bird Chronicle* (1994–5), where it serves as the setting for a similar soul-searching. (The funny thing is that a hidden well was mentioned in passing in Murakami's earlier novel *Norwegian Wood* [1987], which caused the hero to briefly fear falling down into it.)

These, then, are four influences evident in "Haibane

Renmei": ABe's sorrow is palpable yet enigmatic in details; "bad girl" angel posters of the same time frame provide much of the look and character motivation for the series; an indy short "This Guy Is Falling" contributes toward a vibrant opening theme; and novels by Japan's most famous living author give a map of the town and a well for contemplation.

•

"Planetes": Contrasting the Manga and the Anime

The "Planetes" manga was published in two bursts: episodes 1 to 11 in 2001; episodes 12 to 16 in 2003. The "Planetes" anime had 26 episodes, two seasons, and originally aired from 2003 to 2004.

Comparing the manga to the anime, the first immediate difference is that the order of the episodes in the manga was dramatically reshuffled for the anime.

First a table to show the manga side of things:

Manga	Action	Anime Episode
1. A Stardust Sky	Yuri finds compass.	10. A Sky of Stardust
2. A Girl From Beyond Earth	Nono and Harry Roland in the Moon hospital.	7. Extraterrestrial Girl
3. A Cigarette under Starlight	Fee's adventure with smoke-room bombings.	12. A Modest Request
4. Scenery for a Rocket	Yuri. Wise man. Meets Hachi's family.	13. Scenery With a Rocket
5. Ignition	Hachi's space sickness and psychological darkness.	16. Ignition

Manga	Action	Anime Episode
6. Running Man	Goro hides on the station, then joins the Jupiter mission.	17. His Reasons
7. Tanabe	Tanabe arrives as replacement for Hachi. Space coffin.	3. Return Trajectory
8. A Black Flower Named Sakinohara (Part 1)	The testing of crew applicants for the Jupiter mission. Hakim bombs the Jupiter ship.	21. Tandem Mirror
9. A Black Flower Named Sakinohara (Part 2)	Fight against Space Defense Force on Moon.	24. Love
10. Lost Souls	Hachi carries guy across Moon.	24. Love
11. Spacibo	The guy Hachi carried is out of the Jupiter mission. Hachi goes home, rides bicycle, and falls into ocean.	25. The Lost
12. A Cat in the Evening	Testing Hachi and Sally. Press meeting where Hachi spaces out. White cat as a Hachi hallucination.	(Press meeting used in anime ep. 25.)
13. Windmill-ville	Origins of Ai Tanabe.	N.a.

Manga	Action	Anime Episode
14. Boy and Girl	A furry humanoid as another Hachi hallucination. Sally tries to seduce Hachi for health reasons.	(Furry used in episode 17 as corporate mascot and doll.)
15. A Day of Kyakurai	Hachi goes to Earth, visits Ai Tanabe's house.	25. The Lost
16. Hachimaki	In orbit again, Hachi proposes to Ai via shiritori.	26. And the Days We Chance Upon. . .

Next a table to show the anime side of things:

Anime Episode	Manga	Anime Action
1. Outside the Atmosphere	N.a.	(Opening sequence hints at manga ep. 1 / anime ep. 10.) Ai Tanabe arrives (some elements of manga ep. 7).
2. Like a Dream	N.a.	Hachi's dream of his own spaceship.
3. Return Trajectory	7. Tanabe	Space coffin.
7. Extra-terrestrial Girl	2. A Girl From Be-yond Earth	Nono and Harry Roland in Moon hospital.
8. A Place to Cling To	N.a.	Fee is promoted.
9. Regrets	N.a.	Gigalt visits.

Anime Episode	Manga	Anime Action
10. A Sky of Stardust	1. A Stardust Sky	Yuri finds compass.
11. Boundary Line	N.a.	The engineer from El Tanika.
12. A Modest Request	3. A Cigarette under Starlight	Fee's adventure with smokeroom bombings.
13. Scenery with a Rocket	4. Scenery for a Rocket	Yuri. Wise man. Meets Hachi's family.
14. Turning Point	N.a.	
15. In Her Case	N.a.	
16. Ignition	5. Ignition	Hachi's space sickness and psychological darkness.
17. His Reasons	6. Running Man	Goro hiding on station, then joining the Jupiter mission. (Furry humanoid hallucination from manga ep. 14 is used as corporate mascot and doll.)
18. Debris Section, Last Day	N.a.	
19. Endings Are Always	N.a.	
20. Tentative Steps	N.a.	Claire replaces Hachi.
21. Tandem Mirror	8. A Black Flower Named Sakinohara (Part 1)	The testing of crew applicants for the Jupiter mission. Hakim bombs the Jupiter ship.
22. Exposure	N.a.	

Anime Episode	Manga	Anime Action
23. Debris Cluster	N.a.	
24. Love	9. A Black Flower Named Sakinohara (Part 2) 10. Lost Souls	Fight against Space Defense Force onboard the Jupiter ship. Ai Tanabe carries woman across Moon (in manga, Hachi carries guy).
25. The Lost	11. Spacibo 15. A Day of Kyakurai	(Press meeting where Hachi spaces out is from manga ep. 12.) Hachi goes home, rides motorcycle, and falls into ocean. Hachi visits Ai Tanabe's house.
26. And the Days We Chance Upon . . .	16. Hachimaki	In orbit again, Hachi proposes to Ai via shiritori.

There are differences in the sequence, and there are differences in the content.

The biggest content difference is that in the manga, Hachi is set to try out for the Jupiter mission at the beginning and Ai Tanabe is his replacement — in the anime she arrives and learns his dream, which then spurs him to try out for the Jupiter mission.

Of the anime's 26 episodes, twelve have no manga analog. The difference in content is adding office sitcom material, and corporate drama material.

The reshuffling helps to make the anime more focused on Hachi as main character. For example, the manga opens with Yuri finding the compass, which is very dramatic but also suggests that Yuri is the main character.

FINAL ORBIT: ANIME RENAISSANCE (1986 TO 2010)

This essay will trace the rise and decline of an "Anime Renaissance" through the set of twenty-seven works I term "True SF & F Anime."

In the course of the following article I will track two anime studios, Ghibli and Gainax. This is not to imply they are rivals, but rather they are good models in contrast, since they started at about the same time, from opposite origin points, and continued on throughout the era in question.

I must also apologize for the lack of focus. The following article was born in mourning over the death of Satoshi Kon amid the context of an industry-wide anime death-spiral. So it is looking at the whole of what I call "True SF & F Anime" from beginning to the "end" and trying to chart how it intersects with economic events in history. As a result it is not about artistic movements, it is about commercial realities.

So when I talk about phases of the Anime Renaissance, the spans in question are periods of time, not schools of art. Each phase begins with a change of condition. For example, the first phase has a change in anime's Production Value to "High Quality," and ends with a change in U.S. Distribution to "Suncoast." These simple, but very big. The second phase has anime's

Production Value being validated with Myazaki's Oscar, and the U.S. Distribution grows until it is maxed out at the end. The third phase starts with the cratering of the U.S. Market, and the Japanese companies shifting back to their earlier captive market.

With all that out of the way, let us begin.

•

Japanese animation has fallen from the commanding heights it held at the beginning of the 21st century, a position it held briefly after an arduous climb of many years. Anime first arrived in the USA in the 1960s, with such TV shows as "Astro Boy," "Gigantor," "Kimba the White Lion," and "Speed Racer." These cartoons created an initial splash and quickly became an enduring part of the pop culture, but then things quieted down. Decades later, anime went through a process, a renaissance that transformed a national art form. Throughout the world, generic terms like "animation" and "cartoons" were replaced with the Japanese term "anime" as a brand name for a specific type. The rise of anime during this second wave was incremental, and while the decline from 2006 has been steep, still there remained some hope of a rebound until the unexpected death of Satoshi Kon in 2010 seemed to mark an official end to the Anime Renaissance.

One cause of anime's recent decline was massive and widespread theft. Beginning in 2001, the anime industry was plagued by Internet piracy similar to the bedeviling of the music industry by Napster from 1999 to 2001, but the anime piracy continued on for much longer. While the problem seems to have been solved in 2010 through licensed streaming video sites (such as Crunchyroll, Hulu, and Anime News Network), this solution appears to have come too late: in 2006, the major anime distributor Musicland (successor to Suncoast) declared bankruptcy due to poor anime sales in 2005.

Following this international collapse, Japanese animation companies fell back to their traditional base, a demographic of hard-core fans willing to pay high prices for products pandering to their specific tastes. As a result, today anime has devolved to niche content marked by pedophilic and fetishistic elements. It has become the sort of porn that its Western detractors said it was all along.

Now that it is over, we can trace the precise shape of what I call "the Anime Renaissance." It seems to me that written science fiction and fantasy was a powerful inspiration at the beginning, and that "True SF & F anime," the fruit of that genesis, was carried along by the wave.

Immediate Precursor

A renaissance is an outgrowth of luxurious wealth and artistic mastery.

In the 1980s, Japan certainly had the money. Japan was the number two economy on the planet, an economic superpower buying landmark real estate in the USA.

On the artistic side, Hayao Miyazaki (1941–) is emblematic. Beginning in 1963, he rose up through the machinery of anime production: first an inbetweener (the lowest level), then a key animator, later directing his first TV episodes in 1971 and his first feature in 1979.[1] In 1982 Miyazaki and a couple others broke away to form their own company, which became Ghibli Studios in 1984. Their first film, *Nausicaä of the Valley of the Winds* (1984), was based on Miyazaki's own manga (incomplete at the time). In a 1982 interview about the manga, Miyazaki cited several Western genre texts that had inspired him as a young man: Aldiss's *Hothouse,* Le Guin's Earthsea books, and Tolkien's *The Lord of the Rings.*[2] The imprint of these

1. "Lupin III" TV series (McCarthy, 220) and *Lupin III: Castle of Cagliostro* feature (ibid, 224).
2. McCarthy, 75.

science fiction and fantasy texts upon the manga and the movie are readily apparent to genre readers.

This is a special moment, a genesis event. For American science fiction cinema, the equivalent is the movie *Forbidden Planet* (1956), which reached outside of its juvenile genre to draw upon Shakespeare's *The Tempest*. For science fiction texts, the more nebulous analog is the New Wave, when authors reached outside of genre in a similar way.

Nausicaä is the precursor to Miyazaki's next film, which starts the Anime Renaissance proper, but it also inspires the creation of another studio that will play a part.

The making of *Nausicaä* required the hiring of a lot of young animators as one-shots to do the grunt work, and within this group were two guys who wanted to make their own masterpieces immediately, rather than postponing it until after toiling twenty years as Miyazaki had done. The rising tide of money met the impatience of youth, and Gainax Studio was born.

Gainax was a company of fans. They were fans of animation, naturally, and giant monster movies, too, but they were also heavily influenced by written science fiction: their first company, which made plastic model kits, was "General Products," a corporate name lovingly lifted from Larry Niven's "Known Space" setting. The first film from Gainax would be the groundbreaking *Royal Space Force: Wings of Honneamise* (1987).

The Nauiscaä/Honneamise Connection

Hideaki Anno (1960–), one of *Honneamise*'s four animation directors, had been a key animator for *Nausicaä*.[3]

Mahiro Maeda (1963–), one of *Honneamise*'s key animators, had also been an in-between animator for *Nausicaä*.[4]

---

3. Anime News Network anime encyclopedia entry for *Nausicaä*.

Noriko Takaya had developed the "harmony method" used to animate the giant bug-like Ohmu in *Nausicaä*. In the director's commentary for *Honneamise,* Takami Akai and Hiroyuki Yamaga make reference to this fact (36:00), stating that although she didn't work for Gainax, they had used her technique. They go on to say that "Noriko Takaya" became the heroine's name in their next project, the 1988 OVA (Original Video Anime, i.e., direct to video) "GunBuster" (36:10).

The film *Nausicaä* was more than just a training ground; it was also a touchstone for the members of Gainax. When they were asked what type of film *Honneamise* would be, they could only compare it to "something like *Nausicaä*" (41:28). What they meant by this is that it was something outside the normal anime boundary of the times: it was not based on a toy franchise, it was not based on a successful manga series, and it was not constructed with standard anime tropes. Talking about the female character in *Honneamise,* they later say, "We also compared her to Nausicaä [the heroine], and so part of our staff had that image in mind" (1:09:35).

The First Phase

- 1986: *Castle in the Sky*
- 1987: *Wings of Honneamise*
- 1988: *My Neighbor Totoro*
- 1989: *Kiki's Delivery Service*
- 1992: *Porco Rosso*

The first phase is dominated by Miyazaki. My list shows one title per year for five years in a row, then a brief break before the sixth title.

Castle in the Sky (1986) is based on Miyazaki's original

---

4. Anime News Network anime encyclopedia entry for *Nausicaä.*

ideas drawn from *Gulliver's Travels,* strongly influenced by *Treasure Island,* and seasoned with the sensibilities of Jules Verne. *Castle* is thus a science fiction tale with a veneer of fantasy, a sort of steampunk before the word had been coined, and it sets the standard for Ghibli films to come.

Gainax's *Wings of Honneamise* (1987) is inspired by the real space programs of both the USA and the USSR, as well as the narrative of the movie *The Right Stuff* (1983). As the first feature from a new company, its birth was bold: Gainax started with a four-minute pilot film, in essence a trailer for the movie, which they showed to prospective investors. Bandai, a toy company, paid them a record sum to make the full feature.[5]

(This wasn't the first time a toy company had invested in anime outside a toy franchise. In the 1970s, Sanrio, maker of Hello Kitty, had tried *Metamorphoses,* a feature with lavish production in the style of Disney's *Fantasia* [1940]. It came out soon after *Star Wars* but quickly vanished without making an impact.)

My Neighbor Totoro (1988) is another Miyazaki original, this time showing influences from European fairy tales and Lewis Carroll's *Alice in Wonderland. Kiki's Delivery Service* (1989) is based upon a Japanese young adult fantasy novel. *Porco Rosso* (1992) grew out of a very short manga by Miyazaki about a flying Italian pig between the World Wars, a cross between Hemingway and *Magnificent Men in Their Flying Machines.*

It is interesting that the Japanese economic bubble burst in 1990, right in the hiccup period of this segment. In purely economic terms, a forecaster at the time might have reasonably supposed that the Anime Renaissance would be stopped in its tracks at just that point.

---

5. *Honneamise* had "a budget of over eight hundred million yen (approximately $8 million U.S.) . . . at the time, the largest budget ever for a Japanese animated film," *Honneamise* DVD insert card, back page.

While there is no question that Japan spent the next twenty years in economic limbo, still there were a couple of forces that preserved the anime industry. Philosophically, Japan had been looking ahead to the predicted "post-industrial economy," and if the country couldn't be Asia's banking superpower (*à la* Switzerland), then perhaps it could be its entertainment capital (*à la* Hollywood). And the anime artists existed and were producing.

Japanese industry invested more heavily into anime, followed by the Japanese government.

On the American side, anime distribution gradually grew during this time. Initially anime could only be found at specialty shops, but ultimately anime took entire aisles at big box outlets. An article from *Billboard,* headlined "Anime Finds Mainstream Niche," marks this transition in 1996: "Japanese animation . . . is moving from the retail periphery to the main aisles . . . . Suncoast Motion Pictures discovered anime's strength a couple of years ago . . . Others, such as Borders and Best Buy, have since caught the fever."[6]

The Second Phase

- 1997: *Princess Mononoke*
- 1998/99: "Cowboy Bebop"
- 2000: "FLCL," "NieA Under Seven"
- 2001: "Boogiepop Phantom," *Millennium Actress, Spirited Away*
- 2002: "Haibane Renmei"
- 2003: "Planetes," "Voices of a Distant Star," *Tokyo Godfathers*
- 2004: "Paranoia Agent"

6. *Billboard,* October 5, 1996 "Anime Finds Mainstream Niche," (71).

- 2005: "Mushi-shi"
- 2006: *Paprika*, "Suzumiya," *Girl Who Leapt Through Time*

The second phase begins with Miyazaki's darkest film, *Princess Mononoke* (1997), an original historical fantasy with strong ties to his earlier *Nausicaä*. Then the TV series "Cowboy BeBop" (1998–99) brings style and panache to the space bounty hunter subgenre, after which the floodgates seem to open. Gainax, after some huge commercial success, returns to my radar with the madcap "coming of age" OVA series "FLCL" (2000), and a new rising star Yoshitoshi ABe (1971–) creates the "alien roommate" comedy series "NieA under Seven" (2000).

2001 is a banner year. Miyazaki's *Spirited Away*, another original, would win an Oscar, showing a huge acceptance for anime in the USA. The TV series "Boogiepop Phantom" is semi-original — the Boogiepop franchise was based on a series of young adult horror novels, and "Boogiepop Phantom" is a bridge across a gap existing between the first two books. Satoshi Kon (1963–2010), who was already considered to be "anime's Alfred Hitchcock" for the psychological thriller *Perfect Blue* (1997), delivers *Millennium Actress* and thereby vaults to the highest rank. (Kon's career track was somewhere between the Miyazaki experience and the Gainax experience: he worked his way up in professional projects, the first one being released in 1991, yet a scant six years later he completed directing his first feature, *Perfect Blue*. Kon was employed by the animation studio Madhouse. Established in 1972, this studio had long worked on TV shows and provided support for other studios, including contributing animation for Miyazaki's *My Neighbor Totoro* and *Spirited Away*. Beginning in 2001, Madhouse became the source of eight "True SF & F anime" titles, the most from a single studio.)

In 2002, Yoshitoshi ABe scores another hit with TV series "Haibane Renmei," an original fantasy that mines a lot of setting, scenario, and set pieces from the work of best-selling Japanese author Haruki Murakami. Murakami, perhaps the best known of contemporary Japanese novelists, is famous for his "genre-bending" works. In particular, *Hardboiled Wonderland and the End of the World* (1985) combines (or technically "alternates between") the noir detective novel and the tender wonder of a quiet fantasy town. This fantasy town is imported largely intact into "Haibane Renmei," and further bits (involving birds and dry wells) are lifted from Murakami's later novel *The Wind-up Bird Chronicles* (1997).

A second banner year, 2003 sees a return to space with the TV series "Planetes," based on a manga about space-junk garbage men, and the short OVA "Voices of a Distant Star." Satoshi Kon gives us the movie *Tokyo Godfathers,* which seems to be a retelling of a Ford Western set in modern Tokyo, but in fact it has an additional twist for being in the style of a Capra Christmas film. Thus, it amounts to a mash-up of *Three Godfathers* and *It's a Wonderful Life.*

Kon follows this warm and fuzzy film with the dark and searing TV series "Paranoia Agent" (2004). It is original — in fact, Kon said it was made up of scraps he couldn't use in his previous films.

The next year brings the TV series "Mushi-shi" (2005), a historical fantasy based on a manga. Genre readers may recognize a pre-Cthulhu Lovecraft in its weird ecology of invisible bug-like creatures that interact with humans in mysterious ways.

2006 is a third banner year. Kon realizes a long held ambition by bringing a favorite science fiction novel to the silver screen: *Paprika.* The book came from a Japanese giant of genre, Yasutaka Tsutsui. Madhouse also releases a second feature based on a Tsutsui work, *The Girl Who Leapt Through Time,* this one from rising director Mamoru Hosoda (1967–).

That would be enough for a remarkable year, but then

there is the TV series "The Melancholy of Haruhi Suzumiya." Based upon a young adult SF novel series, *Suzumiya* arrives like a supernova, triggering an unprecedented enthusiasm that jumps the banks of anime fandom and sweep through the general public. And like a supernova, perhaps it signaled the end.

The Third Phase

- 2007: "Rocket Girls"
- 2008: *Ponyo on the Cliff*
- 2009: "Suzumiya" season 2, *Summer Wars*
- 2010: "Suzumiya" movie, "The Tatami Galaxy"

External economic events come fast and hard in the third period. The American anime market implodes in 2006, and a world financial crisis begins in 2007, further reducing the international appetite for anime. America appears to be slipping into a Japanese-style long recession, and the Japanese anime industry downshifts to the lowest common denominator.

Despite all this doom, gloom, and degradation, a trickle of titles still makes it to the list.

"Rocket Girls" (2007), a TV series based on a Japanese novel, continues the hard SF tradition of *Honneamise* and "Planetes" by adding more comedy and more girls. Specifically schoolgirls. While this might sound like another excuse for exploitation, in reality it is a moving tale of heroism in the face of bureaucratic bungling.

Miyazaki's original movie *Ponyo on the Cliff* (2008) is a triumphant return, mixing Hans Christian Anderson's "The Little Mermaid" with American animation of the past (including Disney's *The Sorcerer's Apprentice* segment from *Fantasia)* and Miyazaki's earlier *Panda Go Panda* (1973).

The second season of "The Melancholy of Haruhi Suzumiya" (2009) begins with the same magic as the first season, but then it powers into a controversial arc that is brutal on the viewers. This by itself seems to be a shift from "velvet glove" to "iron fist," a signal that the Golden Age is over. In contrast, Madhouse releases another movie by Mamoru Hosoda, *Summer Wars* (2009), which is a charming "Kon-meets-Miyazaki" deal, with cyberspace, too.

The next year brings the movie *The Disappearance of Haruhi Suzumiya*, a powerful third act in the anime franchise that in some ways makes up for the rough treatment across the middle of the second season. Madhouse continues to amaze and delight, this time with "The Tatami Galaxy," a TV series based on a Japanese novel. Imagine a "crazy college roommates" story crossed with *Groundhog Day,* as filmed by a French director like Alain Resnais (*Last Year at Marienbad*) or Luc Besson (*The Fifth Element*).

•

The sudden loss of Satoshi Kon to pancreatic cancer in August of 2010 feels like the end of the Anime Renaissance, but must it be?

The talent is still there; I have no doubt of that. There are a few qualifiers, however. First, the Anime Renaissance has been going for twenty-four years now, a literal generation. A lot of the animation grunt work has been outsourced, so it is becoming less likely for a Miyazaki-style track up from the bottom. Add to this the fact that Japan's population is graying out and shrinking.

In addition to the talent, a renaissance needs economic muscle, and Japan, after twenty long years of what was supposed to be just one lost decade, has finally ceded the "world's number two economy" crown to China. Can the number three economy sustain the anime renaissance?

On the American side the general feeling among anime fans seems to be that anime is more or less over: it was an economic bubble, a Japanese "bet the farm" gamble that did not pay off. The enthusiasm of mainstream America for anime was just a fad whose time has now passed. But perhaps the drastic reduction of Internet anime piracy will provide enough of a boost to allow a new movement of creativity.

Year	Title	Source	Studio
2010	Suzumiya movie	Novel	Kyoto Anime
	The Tatami Galaxy (TV)	Novel	Madhouse
2009	Suzumiya season 2 (TV)	Novel	Kyoto Anime
	Summer Wars	Original	Madhouse
2008	Ponyo on the Cliff	Fairy tale	Studio Ghibli
2007	Rocket Girls	Novel	Mook Animation
2006	Paprika	Novel	Madhouse
	Suzumiya season 1 (TV)	Novel series	Kyoto Anime
	Girl Who Leapt Through Time	Novel	Madhouse
2005	Mushi-shi (TV)	Manga	Artland
2004	Paranoia Agent (TV)	Original	Madhouse

Year	Title	Source	Studio
2003	Planetes (TV)	Manga	Sunrise
	Voices of a Distant Star (OVA)	Original	CoMix Wave
	Tokyo Godfathers	USA cinema	Madhouse
2002	Haibane Renmei (TV)	Original	Radix
2001	Boogiepop Phantom (TV)	Novel series	Madhouse
	Millennium Actress	Japanese cinema	Madhouse
	Spirited Away	Original	Studio Ghibli
2000	FLCL (OVA)	Original	Gainax
	NieA Under Seven (TV)	Original	Genco
1998–99	Cowboy Bebop (TV)	Original	Sunrise
1997	Princess Mononoke	Original	Studio Ghibli
1992	Porco Rosso	Manga	Studio Ghibli
1989	Kiki's Delivery Service	Novel	Studio Ghibli

Year	Title	Source	Studio
1988	My Neighbor Totoro	Original	Studio Ghibli
1987	Wings of Honneamise	Original	Gainax
1986	Castle in the Sky	Original	Studio Ghibli

•

Sources

Anime News Network (encyclopedias on anime and manga), online at http://www.animenewsnetwork.com/encyclopedia.

McCarthy, Helen. *Hayao Miyazaki: Master of Japanese Animation,* Berkeley, California, Stone Bridge Press, 1999.

Royal Space Force: The Wings of Honneamise, DVD, Manga Video, 2000.

64

V

W

Z

ABOUT THE AUTHOR

Michael Andre-Driussi wrote a genre reference book, *Lexicon Urthus*, that became a finalist for a World Fantasy Award back in the twentieth century. His articles and reviews have appeared in such venues as *Extrapolation*, *Foundations*, and *New York Review of Science Fiction*. In addition he works at crafting fiction, such that a few dozen of his stories have been published. Many of these tales have been collected in *Doomsday and Other Tours*, *Fallout Stories*, *Old Flames Burn Manvi*, and *The Jizmatic Trilogy*.